The Sport of Sales

How to Become a Superstar Sales Pro

Craig J. Lewis

WESTBOW
PRESS
A DIVISION OF THOMAS NELSON

WestBow Press books may be ordered through booksellers or by contacting:

WestBow Press
A Division of Thomas Nelson
1663 Liberty Drive
Bloomington, IN 47403
www.westbowpress.com
1-(866) 928-1240

ISBN: 978-1-4497-4762-6 (sc)
ISBN: 978-1-4497-4763-3 (hc)
ISBN: 978-1-4497-4761-9 (e)

Library of Congress Control Number: 2012906790

Printed in the United States of America

WestBow Press rev. date: 04/19/2012

Inspiration

My wife, Tinishia Rochelle Lewis
My two beautiful daughters, LaRee and Zakiyah
My mom, Paula Lynn Lewis
My brother, Joshua Lewis
My best friend, Lavell Greene

Some Superstar Sales Professionals I've crossed paths with:

Ryan Rosendahl
Erik Josephs
Andrew Sewell
Lauren Jones
Susan Knoche
Brad Berg
Kenny Rodriguez
Joe Sanders
Corey Jackson
Anteco Cross
Kevin Conroy Smith

"Do what you are supposed to do when you are supposed to do it, and do it to the best of your ability each and every single time that you do it."

Kyle Macy

PREFACE

I decided to write this book, not so much because of the success I have experienced in sales or the success I have helped so many others achieve, but because during the tough periods, I began to recognize what it took to get back on track. I had seen it before . . . and there it was staring me in the face. What I had experienced and learned throughout my sports career was parallel to the experiences and lessons in my sales career. The discipline of sports can have a direct impact on people's sales careers. If sales professionals were made aware of the similarities, these would actually give them a competitive advantage.

I also wanted to write a sales book made for salespeople, one that came directly to the point with immediate action items that could be applied on the very next sales call. *The Sport of Sales* gets right to it and offers pertinent advice for getting more customers. This book is informative, inspirational, short, and easy to read. It offers powerful tools for sales professionals and sales managers. *The Sport of Sales* is filled with tips that you can put to work right now. There are enough new ideas here to keep you busy for a long time!

This book is great for those who are new to sales. It simplifies the entire sales process. It's just as effective for a tenured sales rep who wants to improve or revitalize a sales career. *The Sport of Sales* makes sales straightforward and fun!

ACKNOWLEDGMENTS

Coach Lay
Coach Driver
Coach Luke
Coach Right
Coach Johnson
Coach Carter
Coach Fox
Coach Muse
Coach Robinson
Coach Edwards
Coach Macy

TABLE OF CONTENTS

INTRODUCTION

Warning! Only those interested in making money should read this book. Proceed at your own risk (of making money).

Michael Jordan is considered by most to be the greatest basketball player of all time and arguably the greatest athlete we have ever seen, reaching levels of success previously believed impossible. His relentless determination earned him numerous NBA scoring titles and records and ultimately helped lead his team to six NBA World Championships.

"Some people want it to happen; some people wish it would happen; others make it happen."

Michael Jordan
Hall of Fame basketball superstar

Welcome to *The Sport of Sales.* It's not enough to just be on the team—it's time to become a Superstar Sales Pro! *The Sport of Sales* will show you simple and effective ways to make sales happen.

The title of superstar is reserved for star performers, people who have achieved great success. With that success comes great rewards. Superstar Sales Pros, like sports superstars, are always among the highest-paid people in an organization. Like a superstar athlete, the Superstar Sales Pro is the source of the vast majority of income an organization generates. It only makes sense that the superstars are compensated accordingly. If becoming a Superstar Sales Pro is your goal, this is the book for you.

The Sport of Sales simplifies the sales process by breaking down and explaining each of the seven steps of the sale. The focus is on the process that will improve your winning ratio and increase the number of opportunities you have.

The professional sales training that exists for salespeople today is too complex for most people to comprehend, identify with, and retain. Above all, it's nearly impossible to apply to your specific product. So I decided to introduce you to a way to sell (a lot) that is unforgettable, enjoyable, and most importantly, easy. You will be able to practice these simple techniques right away. *The Sport of Sales* will finally show you an easy way to achieve astronomical sales results.

*   *   *

During my freshman year at the University of Nevada-Reno, I was one of five basketball players who were part of a nationally ranked recruiting class, but I found myself struggling for playing time on an up-and-coming team. I was among the most athletic and confident players on the team, but for the life of me I couldn't figure out why I wasn't playing much.

Prior to one away game in Fresno, California, against Jerry Tarkanian's Fresno State Bulldogs, I remember going out before warm-ups to get loose and get some shots up. I was on one end of the court and several of Fresno State's players were on the other. One Fresno player in particular was a senior who played the same position I did and was soon to be a pro. He was going through his pregame routine, preparing just like me—or so I thought.

Upon my return to our locker room to finish getting ready for the game, I was greeted by our head coach, Trent Johnson, who later went on to be the head coach at Stanford and LSU. He asked me if I was ready for the game. I replied with a confident, "Yes sir!" The reason for my confidence was that I had gone out and started getting ready prior to the warm-ups. I was loose and I was ready to go.

The game started and we were down by a lot of points extremely fast, mostly due to the soon-to-be pro at my position who had been preparing earlier, just like me. After a big loss and limited playing time for me, I asked my coach why I hadn't been allowed to play more.

The answer caught me off guard: he said I wasn't prepared.

Then he asked me what the difference was in my preparation versus the Fresno State star's preparation. I felt there was no difference because we both put in extra work prior to the game. But to Coach Johnson, the differences were glaring. While I was out there shooting around, dunking the basketball, and just trying to break a sweat, the opposing player prepared with a purpose and with discipline. He worked on the moves he would use during the game, evenly practicing every move to each side. He was very precise in his pregame pursuit of excellence.

It would take me two years and two more coaches before that superstar preparation registered with me. The revelation came to me through a unique definition of the word discipline.

Merriam-Webster defines discipline, in part, as "control gained by enforcing obedience or order . . . a rule or system of rules governing conduct or activity . . . self-control." Implementing this definition can put you on the path to sales superstardom, but what does it really mean?

It took the words of my third college coach to help me see why I struggled for playing time as a freshman, why my preparation was so different from the superstar at Fresno State, and what it would take for me to reach the ultimate level of success in sports and in life.

"To be successful, to be great, to be a superstar, you have to be disciplined, and to be disciplined means to do what you are supposed to do when you are supposed to do it, and do it to the best of your ability every single time you do it."

Kyle Macy
NBA and European basketball star (and my coach)

I finished my collegiate basketball career as a starter and major contributor. We won a conference championship my junior year, and I emerged as one of the team leaders my senior year. I went on to play professionally in Europe, where I accumulated multiple awards like the MVP of the Accor Cup in Bonn, Germany, and where I led my team in scoring in Portugal.

As a Superstar Sales Pro, I've accumulated several awards selling for regional and national *Fortune* 100, 300, and 500 companies and *Inc.* 500 companies. I have had tremendous success with sports sales and marketing companies throughout the United States, doing business with the likes of the WNBA, PowerAde, Pony, Gus Macker, and more. Sports have played and continue to play a huge role in the successes of my life. The discipline I learned and practiced while playing basketball helped propel me to superstar status on and off the court.

Now it's time for you to reach your goals and become a Superstar Sales Pro. I can show you, too, what to do, when to do it, and *how to do it to the best of your ability every single time!*

"Without self-discipline, success is impossible, period."

Lou Holtz
Hall of Fame college football coach

TRYOUTS

HOW TO GET A SALES JOB

"If you worry about falling off the bike, you'll never get on."

Lance Armstrong
World-class cyclist

In sports, it's a well-known fact that coaches want to evaluate all the available talent before choosing the players who will represent the team. This is usually done through what are known as tryouts. Tryouts are held to determine physical fitness and qualification. Those players who are the fittest and best qualified make the team.

In the sales field, tryouts consist of the application and interviewing process. This is where companies determine which potential sales candidates are the best fits for the company and the most qualified for the sales position.

In this chapter, we are going to take a look at what it takes to get a sales job. We are not worried about making president's club or being the sales superstar. We are just getting started—by getting on the bike. First things first: get the job.

Ten Tips for Your Sales Tryout

1. *You must have a great cover letter and résumé.* Sports professionals call these "player bios." A bio lists a player's career statistics, former teams and coaches, accolades, and summary of his style of play. Your cover letter and résumé should do the same. Your cover letter should provide a colorful description of you, the ways in which you were an asset to former employers, and the value you will add to your new organization. You should provide past sales numbers, former companies and managers, and your achievements on your résumé. Make sure you quantify your success. Hiring managers in the sales industry want to know numbers!

Sample Cover Letter

My Street Address
My City, My State 12345

January 1, 2012

Recipient Name
Recipient Organization
Recipient Street Address
Recipient City, Recipient State 98765

To Whom It May Concern:

I am interested in a position with your company. I have a BA in business with a minor in marketing from State University. I am not only interested in but also highly qualified for a career with your company. I am motivated, proactive, and enjoy working with all types of people. I am excited by the prospect of working for a company where I can maximize my skills and employ my leadership and resourcefulness in a professional setting.

As a former manager and top sales rep for a progressive telemarketing company, I know what it takes to effectively communicate with others. My experience in telephone sales, as well as my course background in marketing, have prepared me to organize sales start-up operations, create new marketing strategies, and skillfully confront the issues sales professionals encounter in the field.

Based on my success as a sales rep with Company X, I am confident in my sales ability. I follow a seven-step sales formula that is

Craig J. Lewis

consistently effective and highly results-oriented. As a Company X sales rep, I provided large and small businesses with an array of products and services. As a telemarketer, I did everything from setting appointments to selling Internet service via cold calls. I've sold to customers at all levels, from stay-at-home moms to regional directors. I've gained the poise to make group presentations via phone or face-to-face. Through leadership roles in an educational setting as well as in the work force, I have learned to work effectively and efficiently in teams.

All these attributes, combined with persistence, perseverance, and purpose, have assisted me in developing the skills necessary to be successful in any professional sales position. I would like to put those attributes to work for you. I have included my résumé with all my contact information. Thank you for your consideration. I hope to hear from you soon.

Sincerely,

John Doe

Sample Resume

John Doe
123 Road St.,
New York, NY 12345
Home Phone: 555.555.5555
Cell Phone: 555.555.5555
Email: Pleasegivemeajob@yourconvenience.com

OBJECTIVE

Sales position offering long-term growth and opportunity.

WORK HISTORY

Start Date-End Date

Sales Rep, Company X
Outside business-to-business sales of office supplies
- Sales Rep of the Quarter (#1 nationally)
- Rookie of the Year ($225,000 sold)
- President's Club (annual revenue of $3 million sold)

Start Date-End Date

Telemarketing Manager and Rep, Phone Inc.
Inside sales for company clients
- Consistently exceeded monthly sales quota (avg. of 33% above)
- Branch Manager of the Quarter
- 9 Telephone Sales Rep of the Month awards
- 22 program sales records

EDUCATION

Start Date-End Date	State University, Dallas, TX
	Degree: Bachelor's
	Major: Business
	Minor: Marketing
Start Date-End Date	State College NY, NY
	Degree: Associate's
	Major: Arts & Science

2. *Get in the market.* Post your cover letter and résumé online. Take advantage of recruitment firms by having several shop you and your qualifications around. Let family and friends know you are looking for a sales job, and see if they have any leads. You have to be aggressive, because sales is a competitive industry where only the strong survive.

3. *Be prepared for an interview.* You have to research the company. Have questions prepared and bring your cover letter and résumé. Explore the company's website. Write down questions its recruiters might ask, and have your answers already prepared. The more prepared you are, the more employers will take you seriously. Preparation is the sign of a potential Superstar Sales Pro. (Athletes might refer to this as the scouting report.)

4. *Go above and beyond!* Like the superstar athlete who runs extra laps or lifts extra weights, you must do more than companies ask in the interviewing process—that's how you stand out. If they want a complete application, hand in the application plus your cover letter and résumé. If it's just a basic question-and-answer interview, ask to give a quick sales demonstration. If the dress attire is business casual, wear business attire. Going above and beyond shows the employer that you are willing to do more than the bare minimum for potential clients and customers to get a sale.

5. *Express your short-term and long-term goals.* Your long-term goals may change, but at least you have some plan for what you want to accomplish. Know where you want to go and how you plan to get there. This shows the potential employer that you are confident, focused, and motivated, which are all major attributes for sales superstardom.

6. *Be honest and consistent.* Make sure your cover letter and résumé match your interview answers. One tactic used during the hiring process is to ask the same question in different ways. This is mostly to verify that your answers are genuine. Be very careful not to contradict earlier answers with answers you give later in the interview. Don't use phrases such as "Let me be 100 percent honest with you," as that implies you haven't been 100 percent honest with them up to that point. Lack of honesty and consistency are major red flags to companies.

7. *Be flexible.* In sports, it's been proven that stretching and increased flexibility can improve your performance and prolong your career. You should know what you want in a job as far as benefits, compensation, and work environment. But if you're not flexible with some of your expectations, you're going to have a difficult time finding a job. Have a bottom line in terms of what you want before you start the interview process, and be willing to bend a bit if necessary from your starting point but keep your bottom line in mind. Start with high but reasonable expectations so you have room to negotiate. Always negotiate—it's the sign of a Superstar Sales Pro! Everything is negotiable. Everything.

8. *Show the employer how you can contribute to the company reaching its goals.* Tell him or her what you could do in terms of customer retention, new market penetration, and new business. If your skills are in account management, explain how you can protect and grow existing business. Then explain how and why you will succeed in delivering those results.

9. *Speak positively about your previous employers.* This is the 90:10 rule: 90 percent of your comments should be positive and the other 10 percent should focus on the areas of improvement you would like to see in your next job. Turn the negative things about an old job into positives. Maybe you weren't getting the promotion you deserved because your boss was a *bleep bleep*! Spin that by saying, "I felt I had reached a plateau with that company. I'm looking for something new and challenging with more opportunity for advancement." Or what if your boss showed favoritism to certain coworkers? You could say, "I prefer to work in an environment where I feel like I'm part of a team, and my last position didn't allow for that kind of atmosphere."

10. *Have strong references.* Employers want credible people to verify the positive things about you. The more references, the better! Make sure your references are prepared for your potential employers to contact them. This way, they aren't caught off guard.

*   *   *

Before you can win the Tour de France, you have to get on the bike. Translated into the sales profession, you have to get the job.

You are now ready for the team tryouts. Use these ten tips to help you land your dream sales job, and get ready to become a Superstar Sales Pro.

"The most important key to achieving great success is to decide upon your goal and launch, get started, take action, move."

John Wooden
Legendary UCLA basketball coach

AUDIBLE

1. No paper résumé or cover letter? Present a video résumé. Put on a show for your next employer and make them buy season tickets.

2. Ask for a sign-on bonus, no matter what the position is offering. This will help establish that you have value and you know it.

3. Require a fee for your time. If an organization wants to interview you, make them pay for the experience. It may seem bold, but think about how you will have positioned yourself.

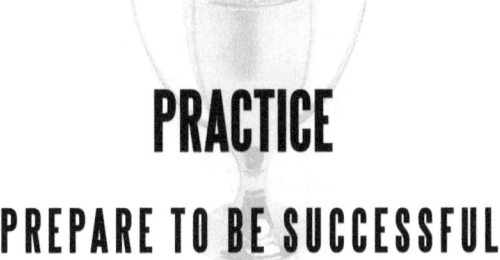

PRACTICE

PREPARE TO BE SUCCESSFUL

"Always be prepared to start."

Joe Montana
Hall of Fame football superstar

"It's better to look ahead and
prepare than to look back and regret."

Jackie Joyner-Kersee
Hall of Fame track and field superstar

"When you get to that level, it's not a matter of talent anymore
because all the players are so talented. It's about preparation,
about playing smart and making good decisions."

Hakeem Olajuwon
Basketball superstar

Like an athlete who's just made it through tryouts and has been
chosen to represent the team, there is only a brief moment to enjoy

the accomplishment of landing a job. Your work to becoming a Superstar Sales Pro has just begun. It's time to go through training camp and two-a-day practices, the grind before the glory!

Preparation for any sales representative is built around three key areas: 1) understanding the basic fundamentals of sales; 2) product knowledge; and 3) customer and market research.

Understanding Sales Fundamentals

The foundation of an in-depth understanding of sales is to learn the seven steps of the sales process inside and out, forward and backward.

The seven steps are:

1.) Introduction
2.) Develop rapport
3.) Set the agenda
4.) Present
5.) Earn
6.) Overcome objections/win
7.) Get referrals

These seven steps are a sales representative's playbook. Just like the book of plays that an NFL coaching staff gives team players to learn prior to training camp, these seven steps are what you need to know before you can start role-playing and preparing for your upcoming sales season. There may be an occasional "audible," but these seven steps are the bread and butter of sales.

The quarterback who can memorize the entire playbook from every position and anticipate any obstacles will become the superstar leader of his team. The sales representative who can masterfully execute these seven steps will become a superstar in the sport of sales. Prepare to succeed. Prepare to be a star!

*   *   *

To execute the seven steps, you must have the skill of listening. Yes, it's a skill! To listen is "to pay attention to sound; to hear something with thoughtful attention; give consideration." In order to understand the customer, you must be a strong listener.

My Pee Wee football coach once asked me why I had two ears and one mouth. Of course as a ten-year-old boy, I didn't have the answer to that riddle. He told me that it was because I needed to listen twice as much as I spoke if I wanted to be a good football player. I should listen to my coaches; I should listen to my quarterback in the huddle; and I should listen for the other team's plays. That's how I would become better.

To be successful in the sport of sales, the message is very similar: listen more than you speak. A good rule of thumb is the 75:25 rule. You should be in the act of listening during 75% of the sales process. The other 25% is reserved for asking pertinent questions and presenting. Later in the book we will discuss the specifics of strong question-based selling and how to ask the right questions to get the answers you are looking for.

Product Knowledge

The second part of your preparation is to develop your service knowledge. I equate this to the athlete who understands what type of team he plays for, relishes that style of play, and exudes confidence that the team's style will win.

For example, on the LA Lakers basketball team of the 1980s, Earvin "Magic" Johnson believed in the "Showtime" fast-break, high-powered offense that propelled his team to five NBA Championships. Although that style was great and successful, however, it was not the only way to win. Isiah Thomas and the tough-minded, defense-oriented Detroit Pistons had tons of confidence in their team's style. It was the complete opposite of Magic and his Lakers, but the Pistons still managed to win back-to-back NBA titles in the late 1980s.

To become a Superstar Sales Pro, you need to understand your company and your competitive advantages. You need to believe in them and enjoy selling them. What you sell will vary from job to job, but regardless of what it is, you need to have a profound knowledge of your product and everything to do with it. Your company will usually provide some sort of product training, but you should go above and beyond to be the consummate professional. Your prospect and clients should look to you as *the* expert in your industry.

Customer and Market Research

The third step in preparation is customer and market research. A superstar athlete knows two things if he knows anything: his fans and his opponents. Likewise, any salesperson who aspires to be a superstar should know two things: his clients and his competition.

A true Superstar Sales Pro has in-depth knowledge of his current client base. Clients can be leveraged as reference points for potential prospects within a similar industry—they can provide insights about what type of organizations have interest in your product.

Knowing who has bought from you and having rapport with them can yield huge advantages in reaching and eclipsing your sales goals. First and foremost, it allows you to add value to your relationship by doing additional business with your current customers. Second, you can use clients as a source of referrals, which could very easily make the difference between being an ordinary sales rep and becoming a Superstar Sales Pro.

Your market research includes having an ever-expanding knowledge of your competitors, their price points, and overall industry trends; your organization's competitive advantages; and any other pertinent information that can help you create the persona of an expert/consultant.

Think of yourself as the superstar athlete who knows his opponents' strategies, strengths, and weaknesses, and prepares with that knowledge. A superstar gives his fans the best possible display of his athletic ability, ultimately creating a winning tradition for the whole organization that is something the fans can be proud of. You have to prepare for excellence and create an environment that your customers and prospects want to be a part of!

This is how you start to build your personal brand and attract fans, not just clients. The more knowledge you have, the more likely you are to understand how to create an atmosphere that makes people want to buy.

"Fail to prepare, prepare to fail!"

Roy Keane
Irish football player and English football club manager

AUDIBLE

1. Hire a firm to do some research and analysis for you regarding your market. Brand and distribute the information.

2. Get a radio or TV spot and conduct interviews of your clients, prospects, and even competitors. Everyone wants to look smart on TV or sound smart on the radio. You'll collect valuable information and build your personal brand.

3. Hold seminars, host mixers, and assemble discussion panels for current clients and prospects.

SCRIMMAGE
ROLE-PLAY

"You can't make a great play unless you do it in practices first."

Chuck Noll
Football coach

In the world of sports, you have to scrimmage, or play "pretend" games with your teammates, to transition from a practice mentality to a more game-like level of preparation. To scrimmage effectively, you take everything you've learned in practice and start combining those individual skills into a competitive strategy.

In the sales world, our scrimmage is the role-play. This tool is not utilized enough by more tenured reps, but it is just as important for them as it is for newer sales representatives. Your organization will probably put you through some role-plays, but you should role-play your sales call with family and friends and even in the mirror or on a video/tape recorder. The more you go through your full sales pitch, the more comfortable you will be in pressure situations. You'll also be better able to adapt and be flexible in your presentation.

*　　*　　*

Practice makes perfect! Ray Allen is the most prolific three-point shooter the NBA has ever seen, with over 2,600 three-pointers made to date. Ray Allen didn't become a superstar by accident. Repetition and practice at "game speed" were vital to his success.

Ray Allen is famous for driving himself to home games (or taking a cab if it's an away game), arriving at the arena three or four hours early, and shooting hundreds of shots to familiarize himself with the goals, floor, lights, and overall atmosphere. That's just on game day. You can only imagine the amount of repetition he does during practice and in the off-season. Ray Allen arguably has the closest thing to a perfect shot that we have ever seen, and it's all because he repeats what he wants to do well over and over again, in every type of condition.

In just the same way, Superstar Sales Pros need to prepare and practice their sales skills continuously. Again, don't buy into the myth that role-playing is just for newbies. You should prepare your material, role-play prior to each presentation, and show up to your sales arena early, especially for the larger, "targeted" accounts.

"The more I practice, the luckier I get."

Gary Player
South African golfer

PREGAME

PRECALL PLANNING

"My thoughts before a big race are usually pretty simple. I tell myself: get out of the blocks, run your race, stay relaxed. If you run your race, you'll win . . . Channel your energy. Focus."

Carl Lewis
Nine time track and field Olympic gold medals

Think back to my description of the discrepancy between my pregame preparation and that of the superstar basketball player for Fresno State. The difference was precision and focus! Because of his pregame preparation, he played well and his team got off to a great start. In comparison, my imprecise pregame workout led to limited playing time and a blowout loss!

Prior to your sales call, plan the direction you want the meeting to go. Explore the prospect's website. Google the prospect, both the organization and your point of contact. Look up your point of contact's LinkedIn profile.

Keep in mind that social media sites such as Facebook, Twitter, and YouTube should not only make it easy for you to prepare for a sales opportunity, but also for those opportunities to find you. It's called social branding. Millions of people are playing this game. Are you?

Write an outline using the seven steps of the sale as your headings, and record your researched notes, thoughts, and any other relevant information that may contribute to making the meeting flow and winning the deal.

1.) Introduction
2.) Develop rapport
3.) Set the agenda
4.) Present
5.) Earn
6.) Overcome objections/win
7.) Get referrals

Invest some time prior to your sales call. The return on that investment will be winning the deal!

"If you don't invest very much, then defeat doesn't hurt very much and winning is not very exciting."

Dick Vermeil
Football coach

FIRST QUARTER

INTRODUCTION AND DEVELOP RAPPORT

We've all heard the saying, "First impressions are the most important." Coaches commonly use the term "First Five," referring to the importance of the first five minutes of the game and the necessity to get off to a good start and set the tone.

In the sales process, how you start can be an excellent indicator of how you will finish. It's paramount that you introduce yourself with confidence and professionalism.

Step 1: Introduction
When you enter your prospect's office, be ready with a business card and a firm handshake. Thank the prospect for meeting with you.

> *EXAMPLE: Dr. Jones, thank you for meeting with me today. My name is John A. Smith, and I am with ABC Corp. Today I would like to take a look at how we can reduce some of your current costs and improve service to your patients.*

This introduction is direct, genuine, and effective. Of course, you will tailor it to your prospect, industry, and product.

Step 2: Develop Rapport
This part of the sale consists of a series of questions that are mostly business-related. There may be a few nonbusiness issues discussed as well. Your goal is to get to know a little about the prospect, the business, and what's important to him.

Some questions you might ask are:

How do you grow your business?

What do you see as your greatest challenge in today's market?

Do you have a competitive advantage you'd like to build on?

Why did you decide to meet with me today?

These first few questions will strongly influence how you move forward.

The conversation you have around these questions will establish your initial rapport with the prospect. The length of time you take to build a rapport will vary depending on the length of your industry's sales cycle.

You will reach a point when you feel you have asked enough preliminary questions and learned all you can from this conversation. At this time, you should transition into step three of the sales process, using a transition statement that might look something like this:

Transition: Okay, the reason we're meeting today is (insert reason). There are several objectives I would like to accomplish before we finish today.

The first quarter is over. You've made your "First Five" count. Now it's time to settle in and play your game.

SECOND QUARTER
SET THE AGENDA

The first quarter is when you set the tone. You also try to feel your opponent out without showing your complete hand. The second quarter, on the other hand, is when you start to impose your strength and take control of the game by swinging the momentum in your favor.

Setting the agenda is one of the more critical junctures in the sales call, yet it is often left out.

Step 3: Set the Agenda
This is when a Superstar Sales Pro establishes control of the appointment by walking the prospect through how the rest of the meeting is going to go.

> *EXAMPLE: First, I would like to provide you with a brief overview of my company and my role within the company.*

Second, I would like to ask you some questions so I can learn more about your business and how you handle your . . .

Third, based on what we uncover from our needs analysis, I will recommend some solutions that my company can offer.

Fourth, if our solutions make sense, it will only take a few minutes of paperwork and your signature to start implementing them. (Adjust this statement as needed depending on what your organization requires to process a deal.)

Finally, once you've seen the benefits of going with my company, I would like to talk to you about how I build my business through referrals.

Once the prospect has agreed to this agenda—just a simple "Okay" is all you need—you can move right into the first agenda item.

Transition: *So tell me what you know about my company.*

Now that you have set the tone for the game, you have control and momentum heading into the half.

HALFTIME

"Don't give up at halftime.
Concentrate on winning the second half."

Paul "Bear" Bryant
Football coach

The moment was intended to be no different from when Charles Woodson had spoken to the Green Bay Packers in the locker room after they won the divisional title. Only now it was halftime of the biggest football game of his and his teammates' lives: Super Bowl XLV. Woodson had been named the 2009 NFL Defensive Player of the Year and was a premiere, vital part of the Packers. He had just been told that he had a broken collarbone, sustained during the second quarter of the big game.

Woodson began to speak to the team about how much he wanted to win the Super Bowl and celebrate a championship with them, and how they would need to do it without him on the field. He could only spit out a small number of words before bursting into tears.

Only his teammates know exactly what Charles Woodson said, but whatever it was, it truly inspired his team. Even though Green Bay had lost their superstar cornerback, the team held on for an exciting six-point victory over the Pittsburgh Steelers in Super Bowl XLV. Those in the locker room said Woodson's halftime passion motivated them to go out and do what it took to win that championship.

Woodson respected the effort, resilience, and will of his teammates. Holding the Lombardi trophy after the game, he spoke about his halftime speech. "I don't think I've cried that much since I was a kid," he said.

Superstar Sales Pros have to have that same passion to succeed and win. Are you willing to pour your heart and soul into your craft to become a champion?

A Few Characteristic of a Champion

- Determination
- Drive
- Competitiveness
- Focus
- Effort
- Energy
- Passion
- Discipline
- Commitment

"Sports ideally teach discipline and commitment. They challenge you and build character for everything you do in life."

Howie Long
Football player

THIRD QUARTER
PRESENTATION

"You have to perform at a consistently higher level than others. That's the mark of a true professional."

Les Miles
Football coach

At the start of the first quarter, I said that you will hear coaches mention the "First Five." This refers to the importance of getting out to a strong start. In all sports, the first five minutes at the start of the game and immediately after halftime are crucial.

Step 4: Presentation

The presentation portion of your sales call is the meat and potatoes of the entire process, so it is critical that you start off strong. Your ability to give a strong presentation separates you from your competitors and, as Les Miles said, shines the spotlight on your professionalism. You must start your presentation with excitement and exude tremendous confidence.

Follow the agenda you gave the prospect in the second quarter. First, give a brief but impactful company overview. This is your elevator speech on steroids. (I had to mention steroids—after all, this is *The Sport of Sales*!)

Your company overview should provide compelling facts about your company, its history, and its success. Numbers pop, so paint a numerical picture of success. Mention how many years your organization has been around. History establishes that your company is proven and dependable. If your company is new, that's fine, because you are fresh and up on current technology that can improve a prospect's business.

Let the prospect know how many other clients your company serves. There's an age-old adage that everyone wants to do what everyone else is doing. If your organization doesn't have a ton of clients yet, you can focus on the amount of attention your clients get and the excellent customer service you guarantee. Be sure to mention any prestigious awards your company may have received.

Finally, talk about your role with the company and how long you've been helping clients. (A new sale rep with less than six months of experience may want to leave tenure out unless you have previous industry experience.)

> *EXAMPLE: Company XYZ has been around for twenty-five years. Today we are the largest product supplier in North America, with more than 200,000 clients. The company has more than fifty facilities across North America, including ten manufacturing plants and six distribution centers employing more than 16,000 people.*

Fortune magazine listed us among America's "Most Admired" companies, marking the ninth consecutive year the company has appeared on that prestigious list. We also maintain one of the most loyal employee bases in the industry, with a 97% retention rate. Our average client tenure is ten years.

My role specifically is to grow our company by helping companies like yours save time and money. I'd like to show you the services we've provided similar companies and explain the benefits they've experienced from using our products. I've been helping business just like yours for three years.

Transition: Company XYZ offers a wide range of services. To determine what best fits your needs, I would like to ask you some questions and learn more about your business.

The second item on your agenda is questioning the prospect. This is an area where you need to be sharp, attentive, and very skilled. It's your chance to probe the prospect, and if done correctly, you can question a prospect into selling himself.

Early in my sales career, a manager of mine explained it to me like this: imagine that whoever is talking has a bright, hot spotlight shining on his face. Your objective is to get that hot spotlight out of your face. Let the prospect do as much of the talking as possible.

Ask solid, prepared, relevant, and open-ended questions. Let the prospect answer and tell you everything you need to know to earn the deal. The better questions you ask, the less you have to talk. A lot of newer sales reps tend to do what's called "tell sale." They try to talk their way into a sale, but usually end up talking themselves out of it because they didn't listen to the specific needs of the prospect. Sure, you know that your solutions are, so logically you can assume what some of the prospect's problems are. But it's much more impactful to let him actually verbalize his concerns versus you telling him what's wrong.

It's like the young, confident baseball player who comes into the league swinging for the fences with every pitch, versus the seasoned veteran who has honed his skills and displays patience, picking and choosing his pitches. The veteran racks up singles, doubles, and triples instead of going for (and usually failing to get) a home run. A Superstar Sales Pro will ask great questions and pick and choose his opportunities.

One more very important point: *take notes while questioning.* This way you will have reference points when providing the final solution. It's also shows that you are really concerned with understanding the prospects needs.

*   *   *

This question-based selling technique works in the same way that a good sports reporter works. To nail down the story, you need to find out:

> *Who?* (Who needs to be involved in this decision-making process?)

> *What?* (What does your company do?)

Where? (Where are your company locations and where are your service areas?)

Why? (Why does your company work the way it does?)

When? (When do you do that work?)

How? Part One (How does your company do that work?)

How? Part Two (How can we help you do that work?)

The time it takes to gather this information varies from industry to industry. The conversation around these questions should form the bulk of your meeting.

There are hundreds of specific questions you can ask that will be relevant to the "story" of the sale you're making. When I worked as a sales consultant for a payroll company, here is the set of prepared questions I went into every sales call with.

Overview
  → Who besides you is a part of evaluating payroll services?
  → What is the decision-making process regarding changes in payroll and HR?
  → What are the issues you will base your decision on?
  → Why did you agree to meet with me today?
  → Tell me a little about your business.

Current Process
  → Describe your current payroll process.
  → Tell me about some of the problems you have experienced with your current method.

→ On a scale of 1-10, how would you rate the effectiveness and efficiency of your process?
→ If you could change/add anything about your current way of doing payroll, what would that be?
→ Do you foresee any difficulties with making a switch?

Time & Attendance
→ Tell me how you gather and track your employee's time and attendance.
→ Talk to me about any challenges you've had with your time and attendance system.

Payroll
→ Once time is collected, who actually does the payroll?
→ How do you track vacation, sick, and personal time? Is this time accrued or is it a set amount?
→ Who signs/stuffs the checks? Tell me what happens if that person is unavailable.

Tax Filing/Direct Deposit
→ What bank do you do your business banking with?
→ Do you offer direct deposit?
→ Who currently makes your tax deposits and handles your tax filing? (Quarterly, year-end, W-2s, etc.)
→ Is your accountant a part of this process? Who is your accountant?
→ Have you had any problems with the IRS (i.e., tax penalties/audits)?
→ How do you keep up to date with tax laws and changes?

Human Resources
→ How many unemployment claims did you have last year?
→ Explain to me how you handle those claims.

→ Who do you turn to for answering questions about hiring and termination policies and procedures?

→ Who is responsible for reporting new hires to the state?

→ Do you know the time frame for filing that information, and the fine for late filing if caught?

→ How do you manage employee human resource information?

→ Do you have an employee handbook? How often is it updated?

→ How do you communicate policies and procedures to your employees?

→ If you were being sued or accused of discriminatory practices, what records would you use in defense?

Reports

→ Where do you get your payroll reports? Do they provide you with all the info you need?

→ How and where do you store your payroll reports?

→ Does your accountant ever request your reports?

Workers Comp

→ How do you prepare for workers compensation audits?

→ How is your workers compensation information tracked?

Conclusion

→ Is there anything else I should know about your payroll or human resource systems?

→ Do you offer or would you be interested in offering health benefits to your employees?

Of course, these questions are very specific to the payroll industry. If you happen to work in that industry, feel free to use them! But even if you don't, you can see how specific these questions are and how many angles are covered. Use this worksheet as a model for developing questions of your own for the industry you work in.

You will notice there are eight sections in this outline. If I uncovered a need within a section, I would ask more questions to shine the spotlight on the problems we could fix. Then I could "trial earn" with my product solutions. A true Superstar Sales Pro will master the trial earn technique. Ask the prospect, "If I could show you a solution that would fix the problem you just told me about, would that be helpful to your business?" This is a very significant part of winning the deal, because you are gaining the prospect's commitment while sparking his interest in your solution.

My goal for the product I was offering was to execute eight trial earns so I could present a full suite of services during my presentation.

Here are some basic examples of questions you can ask to help lead you down the path of winning more deals.

25 General Questions to Help You Score the Deal

1. On a scale of 1 to 10, how would you rate your current method of . . . ?

2. What are some things that could be addressed to earn a perfect 10?

3. Does that make sense? (Trial earn)

4. In a perfect world, tell me how your _____ process would go?

5. How much time did this issue cost you?

6. How much money did this problem cost your company?

7. If I offered you a solution that fixes x, y, and z, and it only cost one dollar, would you buy it? (Trial earn)

8. How much would you pay to fix this issue?

9. How valuable is your time?

10. What is your plan to fix these issues?

11. Who do these concerns affect the most?

12. By what day are you trying to get these issues resolved?

13. What was your main reason for meeting with me today?

14. What do I need to do to earn your business?

15. How can I help you improve this situation?

16. We usually offer no-risk trials to prove ourselves. What are your experiences with trial periods?

17. Would our no-risk trial offer allow you enough time to review our product/services? (Trial earn)

18. I certainly think this makes sense, what do you think?

19. If I do x, y, and z, do we have a deal? (Trial earn)

20. With my program, you save time and money. How would that benefit your company?

21. This plan will have a positive impact on your bottom line. How does that sound?

22. Can you walk me through the process your company would go through getting started with our services?

23. What issues do you anticipate with switching over to us?

24. This package saves you time and money. Doesn't it make sense to start saving today? (Trial earn)

25. What else should I be asking to help meet your needs and earn your business?

Again, the trial earn aspect of the questioning process is a very significant part of winning the deal. Let the anticipation build up. Continue asking solid questions without presenting the solution. Let the prospect keep saying yes, he's interested in the solution you have to offer. I call this "first-down selling." Get the prospect to say yes to one thing at a time until he's said yes to your complete offer. (One first down at a time until you score a touchdown!)

When you are confident that you have the information you need, it is time to move on to the third part of your meeting agenda—the actual product presentation.

> Transition: *Based on what we have discovered today, there are a number of reasons you should use our company!*

The Presentation

Now it's time for the third item on your agenda: presenting your product. This is the part that most rookies consider their time to shine, but the fact is that the questioning is the most important. A Superstar Sales Pro always spends most of his time asking great questions, because the answers he gets allows him to position and support the product. Now that you know how the prospect will be able to utilize your products, you can start to detail the best possible solutions.

Make your formal recommendation and tell the prospect exactly what you have that meets the needs he's described. A Superstar Sales Pro can make these recommendations with extreme confidence and speak with a tone that is matter-of-fact because the groundwork has all been laid.

Presentations have a greater impact when they are visual. Sample products, videos, demos, testimonials, and attention-getting marketing collateral are some of the items you should consider in putting together a visually impressive presentation.

Although all these items are great tools, be careful not to lean on them too heavily. A picture may be worth a thousand words, but it still doesn't "speak for itself." You need to paint a verbal picture for the prospect so he can fully visualize his company using and benefiting from your product.

Most presentations have zest but lack substance. They are persuasive and motivating but fail to communicate one very important message: *Help*. No one wants to be sold, but everyone wants to be helped.

Your presentation should follow a very simple format that I call FBT: feature, benefit, trial earn.

1. A detailed but concise description of each relevant *feature* of the product.

2. A passionate explanation of the *benefits* to the customer— how it's going to help them. This is super important to a Superstar Sales Pro and his prospects!

3. A repetition of the prospect's own words that verify your offering would be helpful—the answers he gave to the *trial earn*(s) from the question phase of the meeting.

Use your notes and review what the prospect said about his problems, concerns, and needs. Repeat those words back in a question form. I like to call it *instant replay.*

> EXAMPLE: *"So let's take a look at it again, just to make sure I make the right call on what you need."*

Here are eight more tips to help you help them and win more prospects over, while presenting!

1. Stand up.
2. Smile.
3. Be specific.
4. Be energetic.
5. Generate a link between your product and the prospect.
6. Be alert.
7. Get to the point.
8. Allow time for questions from the prospect.

When presenting your solution, make sure the prospect can see and feel your passion. That transfer of energy can help you earn the deal. Superstar Sales Pros enjoy selling. You should always strive for that virtuoso performance. Every pitch you make is another chance at sales greatness. Have fun, sell hard!

Transition: *Do you have any other questions? Would you agree that these solutions can benefit your business and meet your needs? Great! Let's take a look at the pricing. Then I can get you started as soon as today!*

"That's the key to success, isn't it? It has to be fun."

Monica Seles
Hall of Fame tennis player

"Just play. Have fun. Enjoy the game."

Michael Jordan
Hall of Fame basketball player

AUDIBLE

1. Don't just sell—put on a show.

2. Acting/comedy classes will help with your performance.

3. Use a theme or topic that is different from your product and tie it in all the way through your presentation—just like this book is doing!

FOURTH QUARTER

WIN

"It's not how you start the game, it's how you finish."

Unknown

No matter what the sport, the score at the start is always 0 to 0. Throughout the game, there may be some lead changes and there may be some ties. What matters is that you are jockeying for position to be able to win when the game is over.

For one game during my junior year in college, we were facing our longtime rival, Marshall University (of the movie *We Are Marshall*). Their school was located forty-five minutes up the highway from ours, and the game was at our gym.

The game had been going back and forth, the momentum swinging from one team to the other. It was a real barn burner. Not to mention that the game was being televised on ESPN2. Imagine doing a sales call on national TV!

"A tough day at the office is even tougher when your 'office' contains spectator seating."

Nik Posa

A lot of things had transpired that led to the last ten seconds against our rivals, but in the end it was all about how to win the game. Who was going to execute? Which team was going to finish strong?

My team went on to win that game by a score of 101 to 100. I had the potentially game-winning free throws with little time left on the clock. After missing my first attempt, I knew I had to focus in, bend my knees, and follow through with my shooting form the way I had practiced thousands of times. I did my normal routine, then took a deep breath and released the ball.

Swish. Nothing but net.

There is no better feeling than finishing strong and winning. We really enjoyed watching ourselves on ESPN's *SportsCenter* that night!

The fourth quarter is the fourth item on your agenda: closing the deal. This is your chance to win the game. If you've followed my tips and advice on selling up to this point, you will be in a position to go for the win. If not, you may be on the wrong side of a blowout. Either way, it's still important for you to finish strong, because more than likely you will get a rematch with this prospect.

I've looked at sales books and blogs from so-called "sales gurus" that teach gimmicks and tricks. I've never been a huge fan of those tactics. But there are some quality phrases and techniques that

Superstars Sales Pros use to help them earn more business than the average sales rep.

Five Finishing Phrases that Win

1. One of the most powerful things you can do . . .
2. Use my expert advice to take advantage of . . .
3. It is important to take the first step to . . .
4. Use your imagination and picture . . .
5. You can be solely responsible for making your company more profitable!

Other key words to use when winning business:

★ Emerging
★ Professional
★ Reduced
★ Deserve
★ Lowest
★ Simplified
★ Technology
★ Best
★ Easy
★ Exciting
★ Successful
★ Valuable
★ Affordable
★ Opportunity
★ Exclusive
★ New
★ Advanced

In the earn, you want to present the price and confirm the sale. When you tell the prospect the price of your offer, there is one key word that all Superstars Sales Pros use. That word is *only*.

> *"It* only *costs five hundred dollars to . . ."*

> *"The price for our service is* only *$49.50 a month."*

> *"Your total investment is* only *$25,500."*

The clear implication of *only* is that the value proposition you're offering is high: the benefit to the prospect is much greater than the cost.

Don't be afraid to tell the prospect your price. Don't fall into fear and self-doubt. Deliver the cost with confidence. An average rep will beat around the bush. A Superstar Sales Pro can't wait to tell the prospect the price, because he's demonstrated so much value that the price will seem inexpensive.

After you provide your prospect with the price, you simply need to confirm the sale. Here are some solid, winning methods that Superstar Sales Pros use to earn more deals than the average rep. Now, although these may help, the bottom line is doing your job and building enough value during your questioning and pitch. If you've done that, then the best way to win the deal is to ask. Just do your job.

Ten Game-Winning Techniques

1. *Exit Win*
So you have given an awesome, superstar presentation and feel great about the way you conveyed the message. But the prospect

simply does not buy your product for some unknown reason. All of your effort seems to have been in vain.

You pack up your things, apparently throwing in the towel. Then, when you have one foot out of the door, you turn back and ask this question: "Mr. Prospect, I know the presentation did not go as well as it was supposed to go. Can you please let me know the real reason that you did not purchase my product?"

Now, as soon as you started to leave, Mr. Prospect felt some relief. He let down the usual guard that prospects put up against salespeople, and he started focusing on his next task. At this point, he won't mind giving away his real objection because he believes that he's not in the red zone (high pressure area) anymore.

As soon as he does give the real objection, like price, start winning by saying something like, "Oh! So it was the price. I am so sorry, I guess I forgot to mention that the price I quoted you was our book price. Your cost is only . . ." Win.

2. *Roller Coaster Win*
New sales reps make the fatal error of asking the earn question when their prospect is at an emotional low. You never want to earn your customer until he reaches an emotional high.

During the presentation, for example, everything you say and do from the initial approach to the price-savings buildup will bring your prospect to an emotional high, which could be likened to the top of a roller coaster.

Once you start talking about money, however, your prospect will drop to an emotional low—to the bottom of the roller coaster hill. It is here that many new reps will try to win, fumbling the sale.

Before you can win the deal, you must get your prospect back to an emotional high, or back on top of the roller coaster hill. The best way to do this is by using third-person testimonials, painting a picture, and reviewing your prospect's hot buttons.

3. *The Assumptive Win*
Here, you have permission to break the "don't assume" rule. Why? Because an intentional, well-crafted assumption can result in winning the order. And that's a good thing. This is a technique that involves the power of suggestion. Frame your question in a positive manner and subtly urge the customer to agree with you.

Example of an assumptive win: "Bill, it seems to me that you appreciate the benefits of my product, and we should draw up a purchase agreement."

4. *The Summary Win*
You can induce a buying decision by summarizing the criteria you and your prospect have already agreed to during the questioning phase and the pitch of your solution. This technique works particularly well if your service requires a lengthy sales cycle, as it serves to remind the prospect of what has transpired.

Refresh the prospect's memory of his primary needs and how you can solve them. Recap what your product offers and ask if there is anything else that you need to provide.

A summary winning technique might look like this:

> "Thomas, let me recap. You agreed that our
> machine offers you excellent product quality, easy
> cleaning, and reliability. This in turn will enhance

your employee morale and also your customers' satisfaction. Your shops should no longer see noticeable lapses in sales volume due to periodically nonfunctional coffee brewers. Is there any other information I can provide so you may place an order today?"

5. *The Calendar Win*

This is a very strong, direct winning technique, and it's very simple.

Pull out your day planner. Ask the prospect to pull out hers. Then say, "So, Susan, would you like us to start servicing your location on Tuesday the fifteenth or Monday of the following week? Which works best for you?"

6. *The Subordinate Question Win*

With this technique, you are coaxing the buyer to decide upon something of subordinate, or secondary, importance. You are easing the challenge of making a major decision that requires a large outlay of funds. The use of this technique lets you note another individual, or group of individuals, who also benefit from the purchase decision.

An example of a subordinate question is "Who will the new units benefit the most, the customers or your sales manager?"

7. *The Impending Event Win*

This form of winning involved referring to an upcoming event to prompt a purchase decision. Think of your local car dealer or furniture store's commercials—these often feature sales that revolve around a calendar event, such as a Memorial Day sale or a tax deadline sale. When is your prospect's most profitable season? Is that coming up?

You can be innovative in your thinking, but avoid trickery or the creation of an artificial impending event. Stick to the facts and don't stretch them. Have no regrets.

This winning technique helps with the procrastinating type of individual, or with someone who may not have a sense of urgency about placing an order.

An example of the impending event technique would be:

> "Johnny, we have a manufacturing run of new machines scheduled for the end of this month. I'd like to place your order into our system so we don't delay a rollout in anticipation of your busy season. Can you be ready to place your order this week?"

8. *The Direct Ask-for-the-Order Win*

When everything is going your way, rapport is strong, and your prospect appears ready to move ahead—go for it. You can ask a direct winning question like this: "May I take a moment and prepare a purchase agreement?"

This is my favorite. Most Superstar Sales Pros use this win because they have done such a terrific job to this point that the buyer has already made the decision to purchase—it's obvious that the prospect wants to move forward.

9. *The Silent Win*

The silent win happens when you do a summary and finish it with a statement along the lines of "So all I need is your signature right here to move forward." Then say nothing. If you have done your job properly, the prospect will be forced to either buy or come clean with his objection.

10. *The Triplicate of Choice Win*
"Mr. Jones, based on my experience, some are able to invest a little more, around X dollars per month, while others are struggling and can only invest Y dollars. However, most of our clients are able to invest Z dollars. Which category do you feel you fit in?"

*   *   *

Your winning technique will vary based on the complexity of the sale. If you have a low-dollar-amount item, one of these techniques may work well. With a more complex sale, there is less need for a specific winning technique and more need for establishing a relationship and becoming a "partner" with the prospect.

Whatever type of sale it is, you have to ask for the prospect's business or, quite simply, you will not get it!

Handling Objections

> "If you're trying to achieve, there will be roadblocks. I've had them; everybody has had them. But obstacles don't have to stop you. If you run into a wall, don't turn around and give up. Figure out how to climb it, go through it, or work around it."
>
> Michael Jordan
> Hall of Fame basketball player

Ideally, when salespeople attempt to win a deal, their prospects would jump for joy and reply, "Where do I sign?" But a Superstar Sales Pro understands that, more times than not, such will not be the case. You will need to be prepared to handle objections.

Have you ever noticed how a football team will try to run the ball up the middle over and over again, seemingly with little or no success? To the average eye this may look stupid or pointless, because every time they attempt to move the ball forward, the defensive line stops them dead in their tracks.

But elite football teams understand the importance of counters and set-up plays. As the game wears on, the same team that has been trying to run the ball up the middle will all of a sudden run a play-action pass! Faking as if they're going to run up the middle again, the quarterback instead passes it deep, resulting in a big play for lots of yards.

When you try to earn deals, you are going to run into that tough defense called objections. A Superstar Sales Pro will skillfully handle objections to execute a big play—in this case, to win an account.

Here are some common objections:

1. I need to discuss it with my spouse.
2. Let me sleep on it.
3. I want to meet with a few of your competitors.
4. I need a week or two to decide.
5. I like to think about things like this before I make my final decision.
6. With the economy where it is, I just don't know!

These are just some of the common objections you will run across in the field. Usually they aren't the real objections to your offer. It is your job as a Superstar Sales Pro to identify the true reason for the prospect's reluctance to buy from you. Once you have done that, you can address the real objection and win the deal.

You can overcome a "fake objection" by asking solid, direct questions and also by reiterating some of the answers the prospect gave you previously.

Because you've followed the seven steps of the sale, you have already qualified the person you're talking to as the decision maker. So you know who has the power to approve the purchase.

Objection #1: I need to discuss it with my spouse.
Ask the prospect, "What types of things will you discuss with your spouse? This way I can prepare you for any questions he/she might have." This will allow you to uncover the true concerns. Then you can address those concerns.

Objections #2, 4, and 5: The play for time
When a prospect wants more time, I suggest asking a more direct question: "If I may ask, what will change with my offer and your situation between now and then?" This question puts the pressure back on the prospect and usually yields the real reason he is not ready to move forward. You can also ask a question similar to the one you would ask for objection #1: "What types of things do you need to think about or sleep on?"

Objection #3: I want to meet with a few of your competitors.
This is a very common objection. Here is a great rebuttal: "Would you agree that everything we have discussed today makes sense? Okay, well, what would you be looking for from my competitors that I haven't shown you today?" This will get to the root of the matter for sure.

Objection #6: With the economy where it is, I just don't know!
To handle a fear about the economic environment, ask the prospect, "Would you concur that my solution makes sense for

your needs? So with the economy where it is, isn't now the time to implement decisions that make good business sense?"

Once you have asked the probe question and found the true objection, you can walk the prospect through the responses he gave to your earlier "trial earn" questions and overcome that objection. Then you simply need to ask for the business again.

Complete the Sales Order and Set Expectations

So the prospect has said yes. What now? Now you complete the sales order and set the expectations.

Depending on your industry, company, and sales cycle, your sales order process will vary. It is very important that you master all the details of that process. Collect whatever form of payment, paperwork, and especially signatures that you need to process the prospect's complete order. This is the start of your company's customer service, and you want to make sure the transition from prospect to client is as seamless and efficient as possible. It will set the tone for what the client can expect from you and your organization from here on out.

We don't use the word "close" when the deal is sealed. This is the start of something awesome, and we are about to "open" our new clients up to an amazing opportunity.

Once the sales order is complete, it is paramount that you verbally walk the new client through the new account process, beginning when you turn in the paperwork and going all the way to the first day of service. This is called "setting expectations."

Manage the client's expectations and strive to over deliver. On a scale of one to ten, describe a process that's a 7 and deliver a 10. How awesome it will be for you and your organization when you over deliver from the start!

Now it's time for the final item on your meeting agenda: soliciting the referral.

> Transition: *I am so glad I was able to help you today! I'd like to briefly share with you how I grow my business, and how you can benefit from helping me do that.*

OVERTIME

GETTING REFERRALS

Overtime occurs when the score is tied at the end of regulation (the amount of time the rulebook says you should play). You have to play a little bit longer than normal to determine the winner. Every time a Superstar Sales Pro shakes hands with a new client, he's scored another deal, and the client has also scored—the solution to a vital problem.

To win—and, believe me, it's all about *winning*—the Superstar Sales Pro has to score some more. The way we do that is to convince this new client to give us some referrals.

"If winning isn't everything, why do they keep score?"

Vince Lombardi
Football coach

"Whoever said, 'It's not whether you win or lose that counts,' probably lost."

Martina Navratilova
American tennis player

I have found that there are three key steps that sales reps usually omit:

1. Qualifying the decision maker and the decision-making process;
2. Believe it or not, actually asking for the business; and
3. Above all, *getting referrals*.

I have been known to be very aggressive in soliciting referrals, to the point that I have told clients I'd rather have three solid referrals from them than their business. Obviously I want their business, so I use that line with a bit of charm—but they get my point!

Most sales methods do not include soliciting referrals as a part of the sales process. But guess what—Superstar Sales Pros do! Referrals are the most powerful tool in any Superstar Sales Pro's go-to sales kit. A referred prospect is much more likely to listen and believe what you say. Most importantly, a referred prospect is more likely to buy from you. Referrals make it a lot easier for you to sell more efficiently and effectively. That is your ultimate goal, to sell as much as possible as fast as possible! Referrals are a sign of a winning brand, of where people want to buy. Create fans and they will be passionate about you, your company, and your product. They will refer even more prospects to you.

To increase the number of referrals you generate, you have to not only look to your current portfolio of satisfied customers, but also reach out to customers who aren't so satisfied. Why would you do this? Because there is a huge opportunity to gain their trust. Once you find out exactly what their concerns are, you can fix the problems. That's the perfect time to ask for a referral.

Customers buy from people they like, not from companies they like. So to get more referrals, you have to behave like the star athlete who interacts with the fans and the media. Build your personal brand and fan base. You have to conduct yourself with professionalism and charm, making sure your customers and prospects really like and trust you. And yes, I said prospects. You can get referrals from prospects before they ever buy from you. Even if it's not be the right time for them to buy, prospects who like you will refer you if your products make sense for someone else they know. This has really happened to me many times, and wow, what a feeling.

Still, there's no better time to get a referral than after you have successfully won a prospect. Obviously, this new client believes in your offer and see the value in it. Why wouldn't he want to share this opportunity with others? I strongly suggest getting LinkedIn recommendations and even pulling out your smartphone and uploading a video testimonial on the spot.

Take the time to explain any revenue-sharing opportunities or incentive plans you or your company may have in place to entice them to give you as many referrals as possible. I recommend carrying a copy of the referral program so that you are ready to show the details and the benefits of referring business to you.

If you haven't seen a referral program sheet, here's an example:

Client Referral Program

As a valued client of XYZ Inc., we would like to offer you a way to earn free shipping! That's right—*free shipping*.

No one knows the value of XYZ Inc. better than you, our valued customer. Why not share the news? For every referral you make who signs up for XYZ Inc. services, we are going to give you free bulk shipping on your next order.

Once your fifth referral starts with XYZ Inc., we will give you three free months of service!

Vendors, clients, family, friends—go through your contact list and earn some free shipping!

Referral contact info:

	Contact Name	Company	Phone	E-mail
1.				
2.				
3.				
4.				
5.				

These referrals are going to positively affect your bottom line by saving you a lot of money!

* * *

At first your client may feel he does not know of anyone he can send you to. It is your job to help him think of referrals. Suggest anyone you may be able to help. Vendors, customers, prospects, friends, family members, and neighbors can all be possible referrals. Be bold and assertive. Challenge him to go through his contact list or Rolodex right there on the spot!

Try this technique: ask your client to write a brief testimonial or recommendation of you and your product on the back of *his* business card. Keep a card case with these testimonials to show other prospects. This helps your credibility, and it also ensures that you get an actual testimonial—it can sometimes be difficult to get a written testimonial on company letterhead once you leave the office. But I definitely recommend doing everything you can to get a full recommendation for your presentation binder and your company website. And again, collect as many LinkedIn client recommendations as possible. Leverage these by sending prospects to your LinkedIn profile.

Once you have squeezed out every last referral for the day, ask your client to call one of the contacts to let her know who you are and that you will follow up with her shortly. Show your thanks when someone gives you a referral; reciprocating with a referral for their business is a nice gesture.

Four Slam Dunks to Get More Referrals

1. Create a Strategic Partner Marketing Campaign
Every so often, do a customer review to see who or what sources were responsible for additional business you've generated. You will likely find 5-15 main referral sources, ranging from current clients to friends, partners, and suppliers.

Build a database of your active referral sources and develop a plan to touch base with them on a regular basis. Once a month or so, you should reach out to them, not to get referrals but to continue to grow the alliance. You want to be viewed as a resource, someone that others can come back to again and again.

Consider creating an e-mail marketing campaign that offers business tips and advice on how these strategic partners can grow their companies. Make quick phone calls to pass along personal referral opportunities. If you refer them some business, they will love you and make the effort to refer in return.

While working in the payroll service industry, I developed a strategic, niche-marketing partnership strategy. I would solicit smaller chambers of commerce. Once I earned a chamber's business, I would put a program in place to actually co-brand my marketing efforts and market to their members. Typically 300-750 businesses look to the local chamber as a valued resource and leader within their community.

2. Direct Mail/Letter
It doesn't matter what industry you're in, a compelling letter and direct mail campaign can bring in a constant stream of fresh prospects that will have an immediate impact on your sales numbers.

Target your existing clients with a personalized letter. Thank them for their business, remind them why they met with you, and review the benefits that encouraged them to buy from you. Next, ask them to send you some contact information for people who might be interested in your product. Describe to them the incentive you're offering for any referral that turns into business.

There are a couple of ways to increase the odds of the client opening and reading your letter.

1. Send "lumpy" mail. Put something in the mailing that doesn't lie flat, adding a distinct bulk to your delivery.
2. Deliver your mailing in a UPS or FedEx envelope. No one throws those away without opening them.
3. Attach your letter to a customer invoice or report.

As soon as possible after the letter is delivered, follow up with an attractive direct mail marketing piece. It's a good idea to include a self-addressed, stamped postcard that provides an area for them to write down the referrals and that can easily be returned to you. Or the direct mailing should encourage them to call you with the referrals as soon as possible!

3. Send Thank You Cards and/or Gifts
Send a thank you card for every referral, and a gift for every referral that generates you some business.

Thank you cards should always be handwritten.

For gifts, don't send the same old boring thing to all your referral partners. Instead, take some time to consider what your partner really would like. If they are like me, a pair of tickets to a sporting event would get the job done. How much you spend will of course depend on the value of the business, but personalizing the gift, however big or small, will make it much more memorable. Go the extra mile, and write a note to go with the gift. That little extra effort is what will get you noticed.

If a client has you on his mind, it will get you more referrals than you ever imagined.

4. Be a Resource Leader

Build your personal brand. Start a First Class Networking club/group (Start a LinkedIn Group). Make a list of those people that you know who are well-connected, avid networkers then invite them all to come together but with one condition, they have to bring someone that they think the rest of the group should meet. It's highly likely this person will be a great networker, as well.

When highly motivated movers and shakers/networkers get together in the same place, the energy is remarkable, and they share leads like it is going out of style. Not to mention, the fact that everyone at your function will be of the same caliber of professionals, there'll be an even higher inclination to share, due to the fact that everyone will feel like the giving and receiving is balanced, so there is a perceived value that you have created.

"I never ran 1,000 miles. I could never have done that. I ran one mile 1,000 times."

Stu Mittleman
American ultra-distance runner

The most important part of being a Superstar Sale Pro and getting referrals is building strong relationships. To build a successful partnership, you have to make the effort to learn certain details about the person who's in the partnership with you. Otherwise, how will you determine what is of value to them?

Once you have become a valued, respected and likable resource to your referral partner, you will start to see more referrals than Michael Jordan saw points. "Be Like Mike!"

*   *   *

Sample Partnership Package
This is an actual set of materials I used to generate partnerships with the chambers of commerce I did business with. The package is specific to the payroll industry. Again, while it may not be directly relevant to what you're selling, use this package to develop ideas of your own for how to make a partnership approach work for you.

A SOUND PARTNERSHIP

The mission of this partnership is to produce an atmosphere in which businesses thrive. When businesses grow, they create jobs, more people go to work, and our community grows and prospers. We seek to create a community with abundant job opportunities, so that those seeking to be advantageously employed never have to leave the community. We are dedicated to helping the community and businesses realize this initiative.

"Partnering with our payroll company helps their business and our community."

Partnership Values:
- → Increasing profitability for local/regional companies
- → Provide small business relief from administrative cost and task
- → Ignite growth from within local/regional businesses
- → Generate long-term revenue for the chamber
- → Deepen the relationship with your members
- → Keep members compliant with state/federal business laws
- → Expose the chamber to new member opportunities
- → Offer a truly valuable service that businesses can appreciate

"Payroll is the heartbeat of business, and business is the lifeline of economic growth"

Increasing profitability for local/regional companies

Our payroll company offers an array of services that can increase a company's profitability. Our payroll solutions provide savings that positively impact an organization's bottom line. By helping clients stay in compliance with federal and state tax laws, we eliminate the chance of paying unnecessary tax penalties. Our time & attendance systems help businesses manage and better track their employee work hours, eliminating overpayment of employees and saving tens of thousands of dollars annually.

Provide small business relief

By improving a company's profitability, we increase the chance that a company will qualify for loans and additional lines of credit. We have successfully referred small businesses to banks, improving business/bank relationships! We use a proven strategy to team up with banking institutions, benefitting both the bank and the businesses.

Craig J. Lewis

Ignite growth from within local/regional businesses
We get rid of the headache and the hassle of time-consuming payroll duties so a business can take those valuable hours, days, and dollars and focus on revenue-generating activities: sales, marketing, and advertising!

Generate long-term revenue for the chamber
We are so excited by the value of this partnership that we have decided to compensate your chamber for helping us help more businesses in our community. This partnership will provide ongoing revenue for the chamber while benefiting the community. Please see the attached compensation plan.

(Note that I highlighted this in the program materials because it always struck the clients' interest the most.)

Deepen the relationship with your members
An additional communication connection between you and your business clients deepens your relationship; a partnership with our payroll company will add that connection.

Keep members compliant with state/federal business laws
We guarantee state and federal tax compliance, protecting businesses from penalties and fines. We also offer several different levels of human resources service and support, protecting businesses from detrimental lawsuits. Not only are a company's employees its largest asset, but they are also its largest liability. Every business needs this protection.

Expose the chamber to new member opportunities
Our job is to help as many businesses as possible, so we professionally and aggressive reach out to new businesses. We

would certainly expose them to the opportunities and value of being members of the chamber.

Offer a truly valuable service that businesses can appreciate
With 35-plus years of payroll experience, our payroll company provides financial services to businesses, relieving our clients from many of the day-to-day tasks that negatively impact their core business operations, such as payroll processing, human resources support, workers compensation tracking, pay cards, time and attendance, background checks, and more. We not only provide core services but a wide selection of secondary services that any business can really appreciate.

HOW THE PARTNERSHIP WORKS

Current Chamber Members
- The chamber will send out twenty letters a week regarding the new partnership and the value of our payroll company.
- I will place a follow-up call about the letter.
- I will go to the business for a company analysis.
- I will offer the best solution for your members' needs.

New Members
- New members will receive a follow-up phone call from me, thanking them for becoming a valued chamber member.
- I will schedule a free company analysis with the business.
- I will offer the best solution for your members' needs.

Please refer to the revenue-sharing program for the compensation plan. Keep in mind that our payroll company will also watch with a keen eye for any opportunity to push business back to you!

COMPENSATION PLAN

First Year Revenue

First Year Payout= $100 Per Earned Business Lead

❖ 50 Business Leads Sent and Earned = $5,000 in Revenue

❖ 100 Business Leads Sent and Earned = $10,000 in Revenue

Second Year Revenue

Second Year Payout = $50 Per Continued Business Lead

❖ 50 Business Leads Continuing from Year 1 = $2,500 in Revenue

❖ 100 Business Leads Continuing from Year 1 = $5,000 in Revenue

YEARS 3-5 REVENUE

Year 3-5 Payout = $50 Per Continued Business Lead

❖ 50 Business Leads Continuing from Previous Years = $2,500 in Revenue

❖ 100 Business Leads Continuing from Previous Years = $5,000 in Revenue

❖ Payments will be issued after the client has processed with our payroll company for a month. Funds can be allocated to the chamber via check or ACH transfer.

THREE STRIKES, YOU'RE OUT!
THREE KEY MISTAKES NOT TO MAKE

Root, root, root for the home team,

If they don't win, it's a shame.

For it's one, two, three strikes, you're out,

At the old ball game.

"Take Me Out to the Ball Game"
Jack Norworth and Albert Von Tilzer

Ted Williams was considered a genius when it came to hitting a baseball. He is the last baseball player to hit .400 in Major League Baseball. Talk about a superstar who could win!

Legend has it that Ted Williams became baseball's best hitter of all time through his dedication to understanding every aspect of a pitcher's strike zone. If you ever get a chance to read his book, *The Science of Hitting*, you'll find that Williams created a strike zone map that consisted of seventy-seven spaces. He actually took the time to figure out what his batting average was within each space of the strike zone. He learned how to hit seventy-seven differently placed pitches. This is the type of detailed knowledge a Superstar Sales Pro gains about the sales process!

Ted Williams had such a high batting average because he knew more than just what pitches he should swing at. More importantly, he understood what pitches he *shouldn't* swing at—what to do, but also what not to do.

It is important for a Superstar Sale Pro to grasp the complete scope of the seven steps of the sale—not just what to do, but what not to do. Here is what *not* to do to ensure that you don't strike out!

STRIKE 1!

Not listening. Over talking the prospect can lead you to miss hearing something that could help you seal the deal. We have two ears and one mouth for a reason. A Superstar Sales Pro listens twice as much as he speaks!

STRIKE 2!

"Pitching" to prospects before they trust you is the second major mistake. Once your prospect trusts you, you can sell him anything! And because you were listening to their needs, you can be confident you're offering the best possible solution. If the prospect does not trust you, then the only thing he will ever buy is what he sells himself. That's usually not a lot.

Developing trust with your prospect is based on factors that will change with each prospect's needs. Some need to test your honesty; some need to be assured of your knowledge; some need evidence of others having trusted you. You need to determine what is going to achieve that trust in each and every relationship you build. Make sure to ask pertinent questions and listen, so you can hear how to gain your prospects' trust!

STRIKE 3!

Don't sell a product or service. Offer the *value* of that product or service. Most Superstar Sales Pros aren't looked upon as sales people. Prospects see them as consultants. You have to educate the prospect about how your offering is going to benefit his business. That's the most important thing to a prospect: how can you help me? What value can you bring to me? Show him the value and he will show you the money.

"Don't let the fear of striking out hold you back."

"Every strike brings me closer to the next home run."

"If I'd just tried for them dinky singles, I could've batted around .600."

Babe Ruth
Baseball legend

GAME OVER

POSTGAME TALK

It was my senior year in high school. We played thirty-two games that year, all throughout Dallas, Texas. Different cities, different opponents, different gyms, but the next game was always our focus. Win, lose, or draw, immediately after a game, Coach would gives us a postgame talk. We would talk about the positives and negatives of the game we had just finished, and our areas of opportunity to improve for the next game. He would encourage us not to get too high after a win or too low after a loss.

That year I averaged 24.6 points, 12.8 rebounds, 3.5 assists, 3.5 steals, and 3 blocks per game. I led the Dallas/Fort Worth Metroplex in scoring and rebounding. I was named the District 10 (5A) Most Valuable Player and earned All Region TABC honors. I was a McDonald's All American nominee, and my team posted a 12-2 district record to win a district championship, our first in seven years.

The numbers that stand out to me when I look back at our success that year are . . . 12-2! We started out undefeated in our district, winning eleven straight. Then we lost our first district game to a bottom-of-the-barrel team. That put us at 11-1. Because of our lead in the district, we had a lapse of focus and allowed ourselves to be distracted by the disappointment of our first loss.

The thirteenth game was against our crosstown rivals at our gym. A lot was on the line: not only were they making a surge to compete for the district title, but their coach was going for his 2,000th career victory. The scene was set, and due to our letdown from previous game, we had not properly prepared for this enormous contest. We lost at home and gave our rival coach his 2,000th victory, in our gym.

But this time I refused to fall into the same trap. We had one more game in our district. If we won, we would be district champs. I wanted to lead my team to that championship.

When we entered the locker room, heads hanging down, faces full of disappointment, I remembered all the earlier postgame talks we'd had that season that helped propel us to be as successful as we had been. I started to give my postgame talk to the team.

I talked about having a constant sense of urgency, about being focused so as to maximize every opportunity. Finally I talked about being disciplined and working hard to be the best. "We have to do the right things this week in practice and prepare for our last district game to win the championship."

This book has given you the tools to prepare for your next sale. As you continue to reference this playbook for success, you will begin to master *The Sport of Sales*. As long as you approach every opportunity with a competitive sense of urgency and maximize each presentation by applying these seven steps of the sale, you too can be a superstar and sales champion. Master this book, play the game, and become a Superstar Sales Professional!

Sales Call Summary Outline (Playbook)

Build Business Rapport (5%)
Transition: The reason we're meeting today is _____
There are several things I would like to accomplish.

Set Agenda (5%)
First, I would like to provide you with a brief overview of Macro Inc. and my role as a business consultant.
Second, I would like to ask you some questions so I can learn more about your business and how you handle your . . .
Third, based on what we uncover as wants and needs, I will make some recommendations of our best solutions.
Finally, if our solutions make sense, I would like to offer our products and service agreement and partner with your business today!
Transition: Tell me what you know about Macro Inc.

Company Overview (5%)

+ Company overview
+ My role and how I grow my business

Transition: We offer a wide range of services. To determine what best fits your needs, I would like to ask you some questions to learn more about your business.

Questions (60%)

+ Trial earn

Transition: Based on what we have discovered today, there are a number of reasons you should use Macro Inc.

Presentation (15%)

- Mac Pack, Plus Pack, Maxpack
- Trial earn

Transition: Do you have any other questions? Would you agree that these Macro Inc. solutions can benefit your business and meet your needs? Great! Let's take a look at the pricing; then I can get you started as soon as today.

Win (10%)

- Present pricing and confirm the sale
- Handle objections
- Complete sales order, set future expectations

Transition: I am so glad I was able to help you today! I'd like to briefly share with you how I grow my business and how you can benefit from helping me do that.

Get referrals!

TIME-OUTS

"They're a little bit like money. You don't want to die with them and give them to your kids, so you might as well use them if you need them."

Mike Leach
Football coach

Let's take some time out to hear how sports have impacted real Sales Pros and their careers.

I think one of the key things that I learned early in sports is that you always have to keep your opponent on his toes if you want to win. Strategy, strategy, strategy—but not the same strategy that the "rest of the world" is using. Sometimes you have to resort to throwing a sidearm curveball when the playbook says to throw a fastball.

I still use this tactic when in a competitive sales situation. I love coming up with creative ways to win a customer over an opponent. Sometimes that opponent is a competitor, and sometimes the opponent is the company that you are selling to (internal pushback). Regardless, throwing a sidearm curveball or trying something that is out of the norm, that your competitor doesn't expect, sometimes gives you just the edge you need to get the win.

Brad
Sales Manager

I played sports my entire life, so much that I destroyed my hips, not allowing my body proper time to recoup. I was able to enjoy a tryout with a professional baseball team and thought I could make it. I played in four A leagues until I was thirty-four, when I finally gave that dream up. During the offseason I played on a semipro football team and worked out with weights and basketball leagues. I would never give that up. If I were to relive my life, I would repeat the exact same "mistakes" and be happy to be in the place I am at this very moment.

I learned that with every team concept, there must be superstars who can step it up when it is required of them to win the game. I learned the value of being part of the team. It taught me how to handle pressure, when to turn the jets on and pick up others who played around me. I found out how to win both ways: with a total team effort, and when one of your teammates is suffering and the rest of the team picks up that portion for the win.

I learned that I must work at whatever I decide to do. In order to accomplish what I want and need, I must be ready to put forth the effort that is required in order to function at the top of the game. I learned that instruction is there to help raise my awareness and ability.

Richard
Sales Representative

I have been a teaching pro in tennis for thirty-plus years (part time for the last twenty-five). The training aspect has always been gratifying, and the competitive nature of tournament play taught me that my opponent is not the guy across the net, but my own limitations. In my corporate career, while I looked to leaders in my profession, I have learned that my challenge is bettering myself on a daily basis. Every program I deliver must be better than the last. My goal is to push the envelope—my own envelope. Tennis competition taught me that there is no such thing as "the finals." There is always another event next week and another opportunity to improve. The same holds true in the corporate world. There's always the next program, the next quarter—opportunities to improve.

Thomas
Corporate Sale Trainer

I have run twenty-plus marathons, and three years ago transitioned over to triathlons. It was challenging because I had never learned to swim, so now I was taking swimming lessons for the first time in my life. When I am training for three different sport activities in order to accomplish one major sport, I find focus, perseverance; goals and high energy are always needed, daily. Just like in sales. More importantly, you have to be able to visualize a successful ending.

Last year, I completed my first Ironman triathlon. It took eight months of intense daily training. Every day and every week, I had a plan which was put together in order to realize a successful completion of the Ironman, since you only have seventeen hours to do it in. And even though I trained against a plan, that didn't mean that I wouldn't be faced with obstacles (bad weather, broken equipment, etc.) that I would have to adjust to.

When I finished—yes, I finished—I made up my mind to get the Ironman tattoo put on my right calf. You see, the mantra for Ironman is "anything is possible." So every time I face a sales challenge, I look at that tattoo and it reminds me of what I am capable of if I have put the right plan and goal together. It also prepares me for the unexpected obstacles that show up in the sales cycle. But hey, anything is possible!

Greg
Sales Pro & Selling Coach

Playing sports in high school, and most importantly college, has undeniably affected the person I am today. Although I have always had a very strong work ethic, playing college volleyball made me a much tougher and more competitive individual. It taught me extreme mental strength, how to handle pressure, and how to push myself through grueling hours of workouts. It ingrained a competitive drive in me that has continued long after my last college game.

This has translated into me pursuing a career in sales. A sales career is a series of goals, and you are only as good as how hard you are willing to push yourself. Whether it's a sales contest or simply competing against my own prior accomplishments, there is always a drive within me to be the best. The demands of playing a college sport have also taught me how to multitask and work in a fast-paced environment. The mental toughness that was needed to get through tough practices, feedback from coaches, and the pressure to win has gotten me through many tough situations in real life. Sales include many ups and downs, and my past experience has taught me how to push through difficult situations and handle the demands placed upon me. Overall, the commitment and sacrifice that I have given to sports has provided me with the tools, passion, and drive to be successful in sales.

Kelly
Commercial Interior Sales

I have played only football and baseball as far as team sports go. Up to the high school level, I boxed as well. I took away the mindset that "you fight like you train." The sales call and earn is like getting into the ring. What you did leading up to that point is what matters most. I currently coach youth football, and the first words out of my mouth on the first day of practice are, you guessed it, "you fight like you train." I don't care if you are Barry Sanders; if you don't practice, you don't play.

Doug
Entrepreneur/Relationship Builder

I rowed crew for a number of years prior to working in sales, and the biggest lesson from that was, "Any activity you perform in the boat that does not propel the boat forward is only holding you back!"

Neil
Account Director

I played pro hockey for eight years in Europe after a brief stint with LA Kings, and was a pro golfer for five years: one team and one individual sport. I have been in sales or business development in one form or another since then. I learned the importance of teamwork and how everyone within an organization has a role and something they can bring to the table. From the individual perspective, golf taught me the mental strength needed to continue when things don't seem to be moving forward. No excuses—as the Nike slogan goes, "Just do it!"

Robert
Senior Director of Business

I was a cheerleader most of my life starting from fifth grade. I breezed through tryouts until my junior year of high school. The varsity squad was made up of juniors and seniors, so there were fewer spots and more people trying out. I did not make the squad my junior or senior year. Why? I didn't do what it took to be the best in time. I didn't take private lessons to brush up on my technique, or tumbling classes to add a competitive skill to my toolbox. As a sales person I am always looking to learn more and increase my effectiveness. I am in a position where I do not compete against anyone else, but I am constantly pushing myself to be my best.

Also, when I did not make cheerleading those two years, I figured they would be the worst years of high school. They turned out to be the best. When I don't get a sale, I don't harbor it too long, and because I work hard, something better comes along.

Hope
Marketing Director

Growing up, I played field hockey, basketball, and softball. I reached the level of playing four years of Division I softball. I feel that the competitive nature of sports has translated to the competitive nature of sales. Just like playing a team sport, in my sales position I have to work as a member of a team to accomplish our goal, but I also want to be at the top of the sales board and put in the extra sweat to beat out everyone else.

Shantai
Inside Sales Representative
New Jersey Nets

I use my adventure race training as a metaphor for getting better at sales. I get better results when I push through the discomfort. The more often I push through the discomfort, the easier it gets, the better I get, the better I feel . . . and all of this helps me get into and stay in a great mind-set.

Suze
Owner
Natural Element Coaching

Through consistency lies true power. Don't take shortcuts (from a mountain bike group ride on Mt. Tam, north of San Francisco). Keep your eyes and mind focused on the play; don't get distracted.

Susan
Sales & Business Development

EPILOGUE

Thank you for reading my book. I'm extremely honored that you would invest your valuable time in reading something I wrote. My intentions are to help you be the best sales professional you can be. So periodically open this book to a random chapter, reread it, apply it, and tell someone what you read and how it worked. This occasional act will keep pushing you forward to being the *ultimate sales superstar*!

ABOUT THE AUTHOR

Craig J. Lewis is a charismatic, energetic sales professional, business consultant, and payroll consultant, with leadership qualities that will certainly help propel any organization. He is at the forefront of innovation, employing a results-oriented, high-touch, business and sales development model that has people/processes/technology as its foundation. Executives and organizations in multiple sectors and markets have experienced Craig's passion for industry knowledge, benefiting from his ability to approach qualified prospects, cultivate purpose-driven meetings, shorten sales cycles, and generate more business.

Building on his diverse background that includes telemarketing, outside sales, sales management, consulting, brand building, marketing, and leadership, Craig is aware of the essentials for success in selling. A natural at motivating, inspiring, and building confidence, he allows others to set high goals and maximize their ability to positively affect outcomes. Craig leverages his experience in working for and with *Fortune* 300, *Fortune* 500, and *Inc.* 500 companies to deliver high value with substance and, most importantly, results. Known for his sports-attributed competiveness and his constant sense of urgency, Craig lives by the Nike slogan "Just Do It" for both his work and life aspiration.

Craig believes in and exhibits a direct, results-oriented style of business with a focus on sales and sales processes. He operates with transparency and communication, implementing a fast-paced, creative, empowered, aggressive, calculated, and well-executed business model. "It's all about people, processes, and technology," he says. He values his college coach's definition of discipline: "Do what you're supposed to do when you're supposed to do it, and do it to the best of your ability every single time you do it!" This is his mantra, and he aims to infect his peers, clients, partners, and prospects with the same discipline doctrine to help them achieve success and greatness.